THE INVENTION OF THE
ATOMIC BOMB

BY CLARA MacCARALD

The Child's World®
childsworld.com

Published by The Child's World®
1980 Lookout Drive • Mankato, MN 56003-1705
800-599-READ • www.childsworld.com

Photographs ©: Library of Congress, cover, 1; Everett Collection/Newscom, 6; Orren Jack Turner/Library of Congress, 9; Everett Historical/Shutterstock Images, 10, 22, 24; U.S. Department of Energy, 13; AP Images, 14, 16, 20, 27; Peter Hermes Furian/Shutterstock Images, 15; Brady Barrineau/Shutterstock Images, 18; Carolyn Kaster/AP Images, 28

ISBN 9781503816411
LCCN 2016945618

Printed in the United States of America
PA02321

ABOUT THE AUTHOR

Clara MacCarald is a freelance writer with a master's degree in biology. She writes educational books for children. She has also written about news and science for local publications in central New York. She belongs to the National Association of Science Writers and the Society of Children's Book Writers and Illustrators.

TABLE OF
CONTENTS

FAST FACTS

- Location: The lab that designed and built the first atomic bombs was located in Los Alamos, New Mexico.

- Date: The first atomic bomb went off on July 16, 1945. It was a test bomb that exploded in the New Mexico desert.

- Size and weight: The bomb known as Fat Man was 60 inches (152 cm) wide and 128 inches (325 cm) long. The bomb held approximately 13.5 pounds (6.1 kg) of plutonium.

- Material used: The power in the first atomic bomb came from splitting **plutonium** atoms. Plutonium is an unstable element.

- Special features: The explosion of 21 kilotons was larger than any made by humans before then. Two of the first three atomic bombs helped end World War II. More than 150,000 people were killed instantly in the explosions.

- Cost: The atomic bomb project cost approximately $2 billion.

- People: General Leslie Grove commanded the atomic bomb project. Robert Oppenheimer ran Los Alamos. At one point, the project had 130,000 workers.

TIMELINE

October 11, 1939: Scientists warn President Roosevelt that the Nazis might make very powerful bombs by splitting atoms.

December 7, 1941: Japanese forces attack Pearl Harbor, Hawaii.

December 2, 1942: Enrico Fermi controls the first **chain reaction**.

December 20, 1942: A construction company begins work at the secret Los Alamos lab.

April 12, 1945: President Roosevelt dies. Harry Truman is sworn in as president.

July 16, 1945: Scientists test the first atomic bomb in New Mexico.

August 6, 1945: The United States drops an atomic bomb on Hiroshima, Japan.

August 9, 1945: The United States drops an atomic bomb on Nagasaki, Japan.

August 14, 1945: Japan surrenders, ending World War II.

July 1, 1968: Sixty-two countries sign the Treaty on the **Nonproliferation** of **Nuclear** Weapons.

Chapter 1

A DANGEROUS DISCOVERY

Otto Hahn and Fritz Strassman struggled in a German lab. The year was 1938. The scientists repeated an experiment, hoping to finally understand it. They started with an element called **uranium**. They hit the uranium with **neutrons**. Some of the uranium turned into different elements.

The scientists separated the other elements from the uranium. Hahn thought these elements would be similar to uranium. But other times when he had run the experiment, the elements hadn't had the properties he'd expected.

This time Hahn tried a new test. Finally, he identified an element in the sample. That element had atoms much smaller than uranium atoms. Hahn and Strassman had split atoms almost in half.

No one had imagined such a thing was possible. Frightened, Hahn wrote to Lise Meitner. Meitner had been part of his team. When she was in Germany, she too had puzzled over the results of this same experiment. But Meitner was Jewish. Germany's ruling Nazi Party was extremely harsh toward Jewish people. Months before, the Nazis had forced Meitner to flee the country.

Meitner was now in Sweden. She was with her nephew Otto Frisch, who was also a scientist. Meitner and Frisch read Hahn's results. They realized splitting atoms was a new kind of reaction. They called it **fission**. The resulting sample weighed less than the original. That meant some of the mass had turned into energy. Meitner did the math in her head. Fission had made a lot of energy, she realized.

Fission research continued. Other scientists guessed that fission released neutrons. These free neutrons could split more atoms. Scientists thought fission could keep going if the conditions were right. It could produce huge amounts of power.

In 1939, Germany invaded parts of Europe, setting off World War II. More scientists escaped the Nazis. Several scientists who had moved to the United States were worried. They feared the Germans might use fission for military purposes. This group decided to alert the U.S. government. They asked for help from Alexander Sachs, a friend of President Franklin D. Roosevelt.

After weeks spent trying to get a meeting, Sachs stepped into the White House. As he waited for the president, he held a letter from scientist Albert Einstein. Einstein was famous. The group of scientists hoped his letter would convince Roosevelt that Sachs's message was important.

Finally, Sachs was called into the president's office. Roosevelt listened as Sachs explained Einstein's letter. Einstein warned the president about fission in uranium. He wrote that it could lead to "extremely powerful bombs."[1] Nazi Germany knew about fission, too. German scientists studied it. The Nazis had stopped sales of uranium, which was needed for fission. They were keeping it for themselves and out of their enemies' hands. Einstein urged the U.S. government to become involved in fission work.

Roosevelt had been keeping a close watch on events in Europe. The United States was not yet in the war, but Roosevelt did not want Germany to win.

"Alex," the president said, "what you are after is to see that the Nazis don't blow us up."

Sachs agreed.

Roosevelt told his assistant, "This requires action."[2]

▲ **Einstein was born in Germany but moved to the United States after the Nazis came to power.**

Chapter 2

RESEARCH FOR THE WAR EFFORT

On December 7, 1941, U.S. troops awoke to another beautiful morning in Pearl Harbor, Hawaii. Most of the U.S. battleships in the Pacific Ocean floated peacefully in the harbor. Three ships even received shipments of ice cream.

Suddenly, fighter planes appeared in the sky. The red sun of Japan was on each plane's side. Japan was an ally of Germany. The Japanese planes opened fire. American soldiers scrambled to defend themselves. By the time the fighting ended, more than 2,000 Americans had died. Approximately 1,000 were wounded. Thick smoke poured from the ruins of the U.S. fleet. The United States entered World War II the next day.

After reading Einstein's letter, Roosevelt had provided limited funding for atomic research. But now the country was at war. The bomb project became a big program managed by the army. General Leslie Groves commanded it.

Scientists had made important discoveries already. Fission worked best in only one kind of uranium. This kind is rare. To make a bomb, scientists would have to separate this special type of uranium from common uranium.

But there was another option. Common uranium still changes when hit by neutrons. One element it makes is plutonium. Fission happens easily in plutonium. If scientists could make enough plutonium from uranium, they could use it in an atomic bomb.

In 1942, workers entered an indoor ball court at the University of Chicago. They began stacking dark bricks on the floor.

Some bricks had uranium inside. Others would encourage fission in the uranium. The square structure they were making was called a pile. The pile grew.

The scientists added control rods to slots between the bricks. The metal on the control rods absorbed neutrons given off by the uranium. Once the rods were removed, free neutrons would hit more and more atoms. The number of neutrons would continue to rise even if the scientists did nothing. The increase would be **self-sustaining**.

This process is called a chain reaction. An atomic bomb would require one. But a chain reaction was still just an idea. No one knew if it would work in the real world. Enrico Fermi, the man directing the workers, was determined to make a chain reaction happen.

The pile grew taller over the next two weeks. Workers built a wooden platform to add layers. Black dust covered everything. Finally, the pile was ready.

The next afternoon, more than 40 people squeezed into the room. Fermi asked for the control rods to be removed slowly. A machine clicked to count neutrons. The clicks came faster and faster. One rod remained. "Pull it out another foot," Fermi said.[3]

Workers built more than 20 experimental piles of uranium. ▶

▲ **Enrico Fermi was born in Italy but moved to the United States shortly before World War II began.**

Neutron numbers rose and rose. Soon, the clicks joined together. There were too many neutrons to measure by sound. Fermi suddenly smiled. "The reaction is self-sustaining," he announced.[4]

For the first time, humans had controlled atomic energy. Fermi ordered the control rods back in. The numbers slowed. Scientists now knew an atomic bomb was possible.

AN ATOMIC CHAIN REACTION

In a chain reaction, each neutron that splits an atom frees more neutrons. The energy and number of free neutrons keep building.

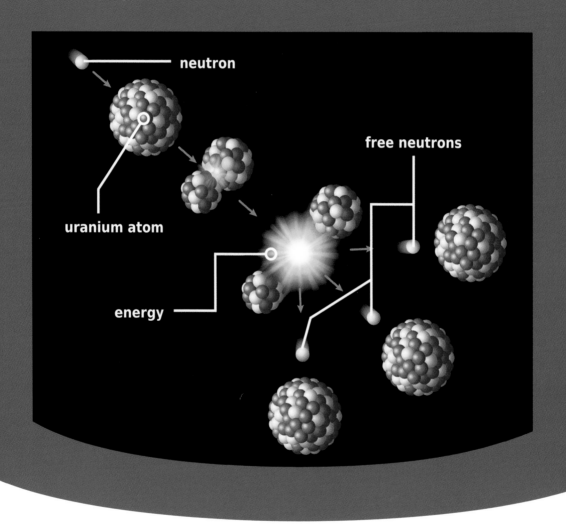

neutron

free neutrons

uranium atom

energy

Chapter 3

A SECRET LABORATORY

On a cold day in 1942, General Groves arrived at a New Mexico canyon. Several men were waiting for him. One was Robert Oppenheimer. Oppenheimer would soon lead a new, secret laboratory. It would create the first atomic bombs. But first the team needed a building site.

Other places around the United States would make the elements needed for a bomb. Factories made plutonium from piles of uranium. Other factories used gas, liquid, or electricity to separate the rare uranium from the common kind.

The project was top secret. Scientists working on different parts of the project weren't supposed to talk to one another. But a secret laboratory would allow scientists to work together freely. Oppenheimer wanted that laboratory to be built in New Mexico. Groves disagreed. "This will never do," he said.[5]

"If you go on up the canyon you come out on top of the mesa," said Oppenheimer. "There's a boys' school there which might be a usable site."[6] The school was called Los Alamos.

They drove up to the mesa through cactuses and thin trees. They got out at the flat top. Snowflakes fell. Groves took in the views of mountains and canyons. Groves decided this was the place.

Groves acquired Los Alamos for the atomic bomb project. Oppenheimer traveled the country finding scientists to staff it. Soon the army had built a simple town surrounded by barbed wire. The United States wanted to protect the secrets of the bomb.

▲ **Little Boy weighed approximately 9,700 pounds (4,400 kg).**

Scientists began planning their research. They held talks to share knowledge about fission. They made calculations and ran tests. They struggled to learn how to control fission in droppable bombs.

In 1944, a bomber took off from a California airfield. A dummy atomic bomb filled with concrete hung above the plane's bomb doors. This was one of hundreds of test runs that aircrews made to prepare for the real thing.

This bomb type was called Little Boy. In the real bomb, an internal gun would shoot two hunks of uranium together. The scientists at Los Alamos had determined this was the best way to bring enough uranium together for a chain reaction.

A plutonium bomb was called a Fat Man. Plutonium wouldn't work with a gun. Instead, the scientists had worked out a way to start fission with an explosion.

The bomber headed toward its target in the desert. Suddenly the plane jumped up. The bomb had been released too early. It plunged into a farm field. Fortunately, no one was injured. But if this had been a real bomb run, such an accident would have been terrible.

In 1945, an unmarked car drove up to a train station in Tennessee. Soldiers dressed as civilians carried special luggage. It held the type of uranium needed for a bomb. When they arrived in Chicago, other soldiers took the luggage and headed for New Mexico. There, a car drove the valuable element to Los Alamos. The scientists would have enough uranium for a bomb before the end of the year.

Chapter 4

A FIREBALL IN THE DESERT

Vice President Harry Truman received surprising news on April 12, 1945. President Roosevelt had died. That meant Truman himself was now president. A few days later, General Groves met with Truman at the White House. Henry Stimson, the Secretary of War, joined them.

Truman had been kept in the dark about the atomic bomb program. Now he would hear the full secret.

Stimson told Truman, "Within four months we shall in all probability have completed the most terrible weapon ever known in human history."[7]

Atomic technology might end the war. It would also affect the postwar world. Stimson advised the president to set up a group to discuss such issues. The president agreed.

Stimson gave the president a report. All three men read it. It told the story of the bomb project. A Little Boy bomb would be ready in less than four months. Scientists felt sure this uranium bomb would work. They distrusted the plutonium model. Since they had enough plutonium for two bombs, they would have to test one.

A thunderstorm lashed a weather center in the New Mexico desert. It was a couple of hours after midnight on July 16, 1945. The war in Europe had ended two months before. But Japan still fought fiercely.

Inside the weather center, Groves talked with Oppenheimer and a meteorologist. The meteorologist promised better skies just before dawn.

▲ **The first atomic explosion was known by the code name Trinity.**

"You better be right on this," Groves said.[8]

Groves and Oppenheimer headed to a shelter. Several miles away, the first atomic bomb sat on a tower far above the desert floor. The bomb had been put together just a few days before. Inside, explosives surrounded a ball of plutonium.

They would blow inward, squeezing the plutonium and starting a chain reaction.

The time for the explosion approached. The rain cleared. At the bomb tower, a man threw the switch to arm the bomb. He turned on a string of lights in the darkness. Then he drove back to the shelter.

The countdown started. Some people lay down with their heads away from the tower to protect themselves. No one knew for sure how strong the bomb would be.

"Now!" a voice announced.[9] Miles away, explosions squashed the plutonium. Fission began.

The observers were hit by heat and a blinding, yellow light. Half a minute later, the shock wave hit. A roar from the explosion reached them. A red and yellow fireball grew like a second sun. A mushroom-shaped cloud rose miles above the desert. It would later expose nearby farm families to dangerous **particles** called **radiation**.

The bomb was no longer just an idea. It worked. The explosion of the first atomic bomb was larger than any human-made explosion in history. It was exciting. But it was also terrible. Oppenheimer thought of a quote from a sacred Hindu text. "Now I am become Death, the destroyer of worlds."[10]

Chapter 5

THE ATOMIC AGE

An American plane crew posed for photos. The men were on Tinian Island in the Pacific Ocean. It was in the early hours of August 6, 1945. The crew was preparing for a historic flight. Tens of thousands of U.S. troops had died taking islands such as Tinian from the Japanese. Japan was losing the war but had not surrendered. U.S. leaders worried that American troops would have to invade Japan's home islands. If so, many more soldiers would die.

◄ **Little Boy was flown to Hiroshima in a plane known as the *Enola Gay.***

But there was a chance that a single flight could end the war. The plane started down the runway. Soon, it soared into the sky. A Little Boy bomb was nestled inside. The plane headed toward Japan.

Colonel Paul Tibbets chatted with the crew. The crew didn't know exactly what was on board. "Colonel," one guessed, "are we splitting atoms today?"

"That's about it," Tibbets replied.[11] He explained they carried the first atomic bomb that would ever be dropped from a plane.

The plane flew to its target. Hiroshima was a city in southern Japan with an army headquarters. As the American crew flew over the city, they let Little Boy go. The plane raced away.

On the ground, people looked up. There was a flash of terrible light and heat. Much of the city vanished in an instant. Survivors found themselves among ruins and horror. Nearly 200,000 people died as a result of the blast. Thousands died immediately, but many more died later from wounds and radiation.

The world was now aware of the atomic bomb. Humans could control an unbelievable amount of power. Despite the destruction at Hiroshima, Japan did not surrender.

Three days later, American forces dropped a Fat Man bomb on Nagasaki, another Japanese city. More than 60,000 people were killed at once. Five days later, Japan surrendered. World War II had finally ended. But the danger of atomic bombs remained.

In 1946, politician Bernard Baruch stood in front of people from 12 countries. "We are here to make a choice between the quick and the dead," he told them.[12] He explained that the United States wanted atomic, or nuclear, technology to be used for energy production, not for war.

The plan he suggested would create an international group to control nuclear technology. At some point it would ban nuclear weapons. "If followed, the world will forever applaud," Baruch said.[13]

But the Soviet Union did not applaud. The nation resisted controls on nuclear weapons. In 1949, the Soviets tested their own atomic bomb. The United States and Soviet Union had once been allies. But they were now enemies. They did not fight each other directly, but they were in a conflict known as the Cold War. Part of the war was an arms race. Both nations raced to build more and bigger nuclear weapons. As the weapons spread, many feared nuclear war.

After the atomic bomb exploded, Hiroshima was reduced ▶ to rubble.

▲ **President Obama lays a wreath at Hiroshima Peace Memorial Park.**

In the 1960s, 62 countries signed the Treaty on the Nonproliferation of Nuclear Weapons. The 62 nations included the United States and the Soviet Union. They agreed to stop the spread, or proliferation, of nuclear weapons to nonnuclear countries.

In 2016, President Barack Obama laid down a wreath in Hiroshima. He paused, head bowed. Japanese Prime Minister Shinzo Abe joined him. Abe set down his own wreath. The two men shook hands.

Thousands watched. "On a bright, cloudless morning," Obama told them, "death fell from the sky, and the world was changed."[14] Some people in the crowd had lived through the explosion. In the distance stood the remains of a building hit by the bomb.

Stopping at a peace museum, Obama wrote in the visitor book. "Let us now find the courage, together, to spread peace and pursue a world without nuclear weapons."[15]

THINK ABOUT IT

- What were some of the challenges the makers of the atomic bomb faced? How were these challenges overcome?
- Why was secrecy so important? How did it make the scientists' jobs harder?
- How might history be different if the atomic bomb project had failed?

GLOSSARY

chain reaction (CHAYN ree-AK-shuhn): A chain reaction is a process that keeps making itself happen. In order to explode, an atomic bomb needs to start a chain reaction.

fission (FISH-uhn): Fission is the splitting of atoms. Scientists discovered fission in 1938.

neutrons (NOO-trahnz): Neutrons are small pieces of the nucleus of an atom. When atoms are split, they release neutrons.

nonproliferation (nahn-pruh-lif-ur-AY-shun): Nonproliferation is the stop of the spread of something. Countries agreed to support the nonproliferation of atomic weapons.

nuclear (NOO-klee-ur): Nuclear has to do with energy created by splitting the nucleus, or center, of an atom. Nuclear energy can be used to produce electricity.

particles (PAHR-ti-kuhlz): Particles are very small pieces of something. Particles make up atoms.

plutonium (ploo-TOH-nee-uhm): Plutonium is an unstable element made from uranium. The first atomic bomb had plutonium in its core.

radiation (ray-dee-AY-shuhn): Radiation is energy given off by unstable elements. Atomic bombs create harmful radiation.

self-sustaining (self-suh-STAYN-ing): Self-sustaining means something that keeps going by itself. To make an atomic bomb, scientists needed fission to become self-sustaining.

uranium (yu-RAY-nee-uhm): Uranium is an unstable element. Germany stopped sales of uranium during World War II.

SOURCE NOTES

1. "Primary Resources: Letter from Albert Einstein to FDR, 8/2/39." *American Experience.* WGBH Educational Foundation, n.d. Web. 13 June 2016.

2. Ralph E. Lapp. "The Einstein Letter That Started It All." *New York Times.* New York Times Company, 2 Aug. 1964. Web. 13 June 2016.

3. U.S. Department of Energy. *The First Reactor.* Dec. 1982. *DOE R&D Accomplishments.* Web. 13 June 2016.

4. Ibid.

5. Richard Rhodes. *The Making of the Atomic Bomb.* New York: Simon & Schuster, 1986. Print. 450.

6. Ibid.

7. U.S. Army Center of Military History. *Command Decisions.* Washington, D.C., 1960. *U.S. Army Center of Military History.* Web. 13 June 2016.

8. Richard Rhodes. *The Making of the Atomic Bomb.* New York: Simon & Schuster, 1986. Print. 666.

9. Richard G. Hewlett and Oscar E. Anderson, Jr. *A History of the United States Atomic Energy Commission.* University Park, PA: Pennsylvania State University Press, 1962. 379. *U.S. Department of Energy.* Web. 13 June 2016.

10. "The Trinity Test." *The Manhattan Project: An Interactive History.* U.S. Department of Energy, n.d. Web. 13 June 2016.

11. Richard Rhodes. *The Making of the Atomic Bomb.* New York: Simon & Schuster, 1986. Print. 707.

12. Richard G. Hewlett and Oscar E. Anderson, Jr. *A History of the United States Atomic Energy Commission.* University Park, PA: Pennsylvania State University Press, 1962. 577. *U.S. Department of Energy.* Web. 13 June 2016.

13. Ibid. 579.

14. Gardiner Harris. "At Hiroshima Memorial, Obama Says Nuclear Arms Require 'Moral Revolution,'" *New York Times.* New York Times Company, 27 May 2016. Web. 13 June 2016.

15. Justin McCurry. "Barack Obama Says Memory of Hiroshima 'Must Never Fade.'" *The Guardian.* Guardian News and Media Limited, 27 May 2016. Web. 13 June 2016.

TO LEARN MORE

Books

Callery, Sean. *World War II*. New York: Scholastic, 2013.

Conkling, Winifred. *Radioactive! How Irene Curie and Lise Meitner Revolutionized Science and Changed the World*. Chapel Hill, NC: Algonquin Young Readers, 2016.

Sheinkin, Steve. *Bomb: The Race to Build—and Steal—the World's Most Dangerous Weapon*. New York: Roaring Book Press, 2012.

Web Sites

Visit our Web site for links about the invention of the atomic bomb: childsworld.com/links

Note to Parents, Teachers, and Librarians: We routinely verify our Web links to make sure they are safe and active sites. So encourage your readers to check them out!

INDEX